Faith

Poetry as Prayer
Denise Levertov

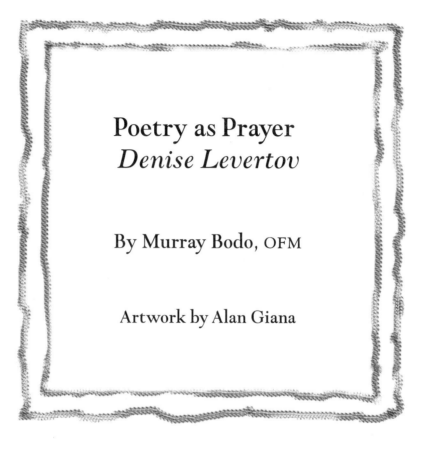

Poetry as Prayer
Denise Levertov

By Murray Bodo, OFM

Artwork by Alan Giana

Pauline
BOOKS & MEDIA
BOSTON

Library of Congress Cataloging-in-Publication Data

Bodo, Murray.
    Poetry as prayer, Denise Levertov / Murray Bodo.
        P. cm. — (The poetry as prayer series)
    Includes bibliographical references (p. 117).
    ISBN 0-8198-5924-9
        1. Levertov, Denise, 1923- —Religion. 2. Religious poetry,
American—History and criticism. 3. Religion and literature. 4.
Prayer in literature. 5. Prayer. I. Title: Denise Levertov. II. Title.
III. Series.
PS3562.E8876 Z56 2001
811'.54—dc21

                                                        00-061114

Excerpts of Denise Levertov's poems from BREATHING THE
WATER, copyright © 1987 by Denise Levertov. Reprinted by
permission of New Directions Publishing Corp.

Excerpts of Denise Levertov's poems from SANDS OF THE WELL,
copyright © 1996 by Denise Levertov. Reprinted by permission of
New Directions Publishing Corp.

The photo of Denise Levertov on page 5 is used with permission
from New Directions Publishing Corp.

Printed and published in the U.S.A. by Pauline Books & Media,
50 Saint Pauls Avenue, Boston MA 02130-3491.

www.pauline.org

Pauline Books & Media is the publishing house of the Daughters
of St. Paul, an international congregation of women religious
serving the Church with the communications media.

1 2 3 4 5 6   06 05 04 03 02 01

*To all my students with whom I have
listened, for thirty-five years,
to the music of lines and spaces,
and witnessed the inscape of the
soul's making.*

Contents

Foreword

When my husband and I were young assistant professors of English in the 1970s, Denise Levertov was his colleague at Tufts University. I was too shy ever to approach her in person, because she was a renowned poet. But I would sometimes stroll by her house, gaze admiringly at her garden (very English, aflame with tall perennial flowers that brightened our drab city neighborhood), and feel a certain bond with her: we shared a self-assured agnosticism, a Jewish heritage, and anti-war politics. Ten years later, when we had both moved away, I found myself gradually and inexorably drawn to God and then to baptism in the Catholic Church. A decade later still, while writing about contemporary Christian poets, I discovered with surprised joy that Levertov had followed a similar spiritual path.

So how wonderful to learn now, reading *Poetry as Prayer: Denise Levertov*, that Father Murray Bodo accompanied her on her spiritual journey over precisely those twenty years, until her death in 1997. Their friendship began when she sent him a thank-you gift for his own first published book of poems in 1977. It deepened, he tells us, as over the years they came to share their love of nature, their abhorrence of war and violence, their exploration of matters of faith, and their craft of poetry. Reading between the lines, I sense the profound mutuality of their relationship: she was his mentor as a poet; he was hers as a spiritual guide.

Who could be more qualified than Father Bodo to open for us the soul of Denise Levertov's poetry? Drawing on his own experience as a poet and as her friend, he illuminates for us the contemplative nature of her writing process. Out of his wisdom gained as professor, as spiritual director, and as Franciscan priest, he shows us how our reading of poetry can become an act of prayer and our praying can become an act of imagination like a poem.

Bodo manages all this with a seamless movement that makes this little book itself a work of art, of spiritual literature. Gently he takes us from commentary on a poem, to a particular lesson gleaned from Levertov's life, to an insight about prayer (how it must lead inevitably to charity, for instance), and back into the poem. And all the while, he keeps before us Levertov's central concerns: the natural world as God's creation; issues of peace and social justice; the mystery of grace at the core of life. Reading Murray Bodo's reflection on Denise Levertov is for me like doing *tai chi*—being stretched out, at each point, into a meditative moment that is at once energizing in itself and also integrated into a pattern that puts one in harmony with the universe.

Everywhere Bodo is practicing a key motif of his preaching: the important caution that we must *slow down* in order to read poetry, to pray, to attend to God's presence in our hectic world. But I'm especially grateful for the section where he deliberately demonstrates this message: he quietly leads the reader through his own unrushed meditation on Levertov's poem "Swan in Falling Snow." Something quite special happens here. Whereas the rest of Bodo's book is *about* poetry as prayer and prayer as poetry, this section *is* prayer—with and through a poem.

Murray Bodo and Denise Levertov join the other fine writers in the *Poetry as Prayer* series, where poets and commentators alike combine deep spirituality with keen intelligence and a love of language. Like the preceding

Acknowledgements

I would like to thank all of those who helped in the writing of this book, in particular Rose Berger of *Sojourners* magazine for her insights and explanations of various aspects of Denise's life and work, and Emily Archer for her careful reading of a preliminary draft of the book. Special thanks to the poet Herbert Lomas, for his generous and perceptive editing of the final draft.

Calling Poetry...Prayer?

A good poem is a work of art, and like any art it exists and has its own value apart from whatever use we might make of it. To speak of poetry as prayer, then, might at first seem to make of poetry something that it is not. Like a painting or a musical composition, a poem exists simply to be accepted for what it is: a thing constructed of words that are the shortest distance between the maker and what is made. A poem is to be read or heard and reverenced for saying no more than itself and not as a way into a better life or an answer to the meaning of life or a way into prayer.

And yet having said that, certain poems, because of what they say and how they say it, are either themselves prayers, or elicit responses akin to prayer. By this, I mean that some poems lift the soul to God either by the psalm-like incantation of their lines, or by the transcendent power of their images, or because they relate a personal spiritual journey. Dante comes to mind as does Shakespeare, both of whom uttered poems that were prayers and who fashioned images of the soul's journey into God. Who cannot be moved to contemplation of the Divine by reading Longfellow's translation of the opening lines of Dante's *Paradiso*?

La gloria di colui che tutto move
> The glory of him who moveth everything

per l'universo penetra e risplende
> Doth penetrate the universe, and shine

in una parte piu e meno altrove.
> In one part more and in another less.

Nel ciel che piu della sua luce prende
> Within that heaven which most his light receives

fu'io, e vidi cose che ridire
> Was I, and things beheld which to repeat

ne sa ne puo chi di la su discende;
> Nor knows, nor can, who from above descends;

perche appressando se al suo disire,

Because in drawing near to its desire

nostro intelletto si profonda tanto,

Our intellect engulfs itself so far,

che dietro la memoria non puo ire.

That after it the memory cannot go.[1]

Or who does not respond to the truth of the human situation in relation to our Creator and the mystery of human suffering when the old and broken King Lear speaks to his daughter Cordelia at the end of Shakespeare's great tragedy?

No, no, no, no! Come, let's away to prison.

We two alone will sing like birds i' the cage.

When thou dost ask me blessing, I'll kneel down

And ask forgiveness. So we'll live,

And pray, and sing, and tell old tales, and laugh

At gilded butterflies, and hear poor rogues

Talk of Court news. And we'll talk with them too,

Who loses and who wins, who's in, who's out,

And take upon's the mystery of things

As if we were God's spies. And we'll wear out,

In a walled prison, packs and sects of great ones

That ebb and flow by the moon

(King Lear, V, III, 8–18).[2]

3

To pray with such lines from Dante and Shakespeare or to be drawn to prayer by their images is not a misuse of poetry, but rather a response to what is already there. A poem does not even need to be specifically religious to lead us into prayer. It can be a simple meditation on or articulation of the poet's experience that invites the reader to praise or adoration or awe. Or, as in the case of Denise Levertov, it can be an invitation to enter the mystery of "deep down things," to echo Gerard Manley Hopkins.

A poet's gift is the exact, unaffected words that contemplate something as concrete and simple as a swan in falling snow and see therein more than most of us see in a grand and overwhelming panorama. With simplicity and attention to the natural world, Denise Levertov began and ended her journey of words, seeking a secret communion in her life and in her poems.

Chapter 2

Denise Levertov:
A Contemplative Activist

The first time I saw Denise Levertov was in the spring of 1973. She was the Elliston Poet at the University of Cincinnati that semester, and she was standing in the aisle prior to delivering a lecture. She was bent forward talking to someone seated at the end of a row of chairs. She wore a frumpy flowered dress that reminded me of something Queen Elizabeth II would wear—just English matronly enough to make her look informal yet a bit distant, too, as though she represented another generation. And to me she did indeed; she was seventeen years my senior.

That evening I sat in awe. I didn't dare approach her afterward to say how I loved what she said, how I felt as connected to her words that night as I had to her poems. She seemed much more removed from me then than even the distance between the podium and the last row in the auditorium where I sat in awe. Here was the person behind the poems I had read and reread, the poems that said things I wished I could have said in just that way.

That evening, I merely listened. And as I listened to the personal voice behind the mentoring voice of the poems I loved, I realized it sounded different from what I had anticipated. There was a kind of hesitancy that I later learned derived partly from a glandular problem which required that she always have drinking water with her. (Her omnipresent water flask is one of my most persistent memories!) But even more than that, her hesitancy was the manifestation of the thoughtful way in which she used words. Denise seldom spoke glibly. It was as if she were searching for the right word to emerge as she went along, much as she said a poem proceeds—organically, word by word, image by image, line by line.

Six years later, when I met Denise face to face after a year of correspondence, my first impression was reinforced: the same indecisive speech which was not actually doubtful, but rather, thoughtful. And now, added to that, her intense eyes with the delightful glint that I soon learned betrayed a childlike desire to know, to know why. And still, as if repeating the flowered dress impression, there was a reserve in her manner. She seemed to hold herself poised in the knowledge that any exchange would not happen with the body but with the mind and heart. Her arms crossed before her, her hands tucked primly into them, looked somehow at odds with her hair that fell in loose curls, almost in disarray. I sensed an inner tension between formality and informality—the intense eyes with their childlike glint, the seemingly solitary figure yearning for solidarity with others, the penetrating presence whose hesitant speech accomplished the closeness it seemed determined to prevent.

These tensions in Denise Levertov made her both formidable and vulnerable. She was formidable in her assurances, which came from carefully thought-out convictions, but vulnerable in her outward persona which gave the impression of a driven person, yet one who probed and prodded from some inaccessible place, preventing the personal communion with people that she found with nature.

Years after that first meeting with Denise in 1979, I walked the woods near her Seattle home with her; watched her stop and look long and in wonder at a caterpillar resting on a leaf; heard her hum lines from Tchaikovsky's *Swan Lake* as she pointed from her kitchen window to the cypress trees on the far shore of Lake

Washington, saying they reminded her of ballerinas. With her, I crossed the border of the Nuclear Test Site outside Las Vegas, and prayed with her at Mass in our friary and in her own parish church. Always when I was with Denise, the words from her poem "Swan in Falling Snow" seemed to come true, "the short day/suspended itself, endless," because of the way she looked at things, pointed them out to me, made a case for something she felt strongly. And when I heard of her death as I sat looking out onto the Atlantic Ocean, that day, too, suddenly suspended itself, endless in my memory.

The last time I saw Denise was April 25, 1995, two years before her death. She had been staying with us at our friary for two days, and I saw her off at the Greater Cincinnati airport in Covington, Kentucky. In the Comair terminal, as she waited to board her flight, I prayed with her for the healing of a slow-growing stomach melanoma and an ulcer. She was wearing black: black jacket, black riding pants, with boots laced above the ankles. Her scuffed, weather-beaten red purse looked pathetic and seemed to reflect how she was feeling, facing two and a half days at Purdue University, reading and teaching a creative writing class. From there she would fly via Chicago to Seattle and her beloved Mount Rainier and

Denise's father, Paul Philip Levertov, was a Russian Hasidic Jew. She writes of him, the quiet Talmud scholar in a Russia where the Gospels were forbidden, and how he found a Hebrew scrap of the New Testament, became convinced about the person of Jesus, and thus had to flee his home to Germany, where he formally became a Christian. Later, in Constantinople, he met a Welsh girl whose great-uncle had lived in a one-room whitewashed cottage with an earthen floor and who had seen Napoleon on his great horse at Waterloo. By the time Denise was born, her father had settled in England and become an Anglican priest and a scholar dedicated to Jewish-Christian dialogue.

Denise's Welsh mother, Beatrice Adelaide Spooner-Jones, wrote, sang, and painted. With the help of the British Broadcasting Corporation's Daily School radio, she home-educated Denise and Denise's older sister Olga until their thirteenth year. Beatrice enjoyed reading aloud and her family heard books by Willa Cather, Joseph Conrad, Charles Dickens, and Leo Tolstoy. She also read them poetry, especially the lyrics of Tennyson. Though an active woman in political and humanitarian causes, Beatrice also imparted to Denise an intensely lyrical feeling for nature.

One may wonder at the poetic influence the words of a Welsh mother and a Jewish father had on Denise. The sound of Celtic speech often imitates sounds in the natural world. Celtic traditions hold that the original harmony of the world is still to be found in the sounds of nature. The language imitates the sounds of the river, the waves, the seabirds, and the wind. The Jewish influence, especially the Kabbalistic mysticism which had influenced her father, was a repetitive reweaving of primordial sounds in the attempt to heal a broken cadence between the human and the Divine. For Kabbalists, every letter and every sound of the Torah reveals God; and one mantric practice among some consists of repeating the sound of a sacred word, much like the Buddhist sounding of "Om." The Jewish mystics also believe there are sacred tones, sounds, and rhythms that are part of a fundamental harmony. They seek to attain harmony with these sounds and rhythms as a way of re-establishing the world's harmony.

Denise, for whom the sound of the line in a poem came to matter so much, absorbed the sounds in her parents' speech; her poems reflect this harmony. "Her breath worked with the line breaks precisely, subtly, producing nuances of melody and pitch," writes Judith Dunbar of one of Denise's last poetry-readings at Stanford University on April 28, 1997.[1]

The nine-year age gap between Denise and her sister Olga left Denise with the time and solitude of an only child who spends hours by herself in the woods. Perhaps due to this aloneness and her unique education, already by age seven Denise had a sense of herself as a person with a vocation, someone "set apart" for art. At the age of twelve, she sent several of her poems to T. S. Eliot, who wrote a two-page letter offering her "excellent advice," a letter she eventually lost in her moves from England to New York, then to Somerville, Massachusetts, and finally to her last home near Seattle's Seward Park in Lake Washington's wooded peninsula.

Over and again in sparse autobiographical sketches about her childhood, Denise highlights *difference*. She was different from other children because of her parents: her father, an Anglican priest who had been a Russian Jewish scholar and was a descendent of Schneour Zalman, the founder of Habad Hasidism; her mother, a Welsh Congregationalist whose ancestor, Angell Jones of Mold, was a Welsh tailor with apprentices who came to learn Biblical interpretations from him while cutting and stitching.

The Levertov home in Ilford was different, too. Unlike other houses, it had no half-curtains or Venetian blinds, so that passers-by could look in past the open side curtains to observe bookshelves in every room, and in her father's upstairs study, a large stone statue of Jesus preaching. Even her mother's front garden, not as primly kept as other gardens, had California poppies, unique in Ilford.

The Levertovs were activists, and unlike other neighborhood parents, Paul Levertov would stand on a corner soapbox protesting Mussolini's invasion of Abyssinia, while Denise's mother canvassed for the League of Nations Union. Both of Denise's parents and her sister worked on behalf of German and Austrian refugees in England from 1933 onward. Denise studied painting and ballet, and during World War II began nursing training at several London hospitals.

Denise's own activism often emphasized the tensions of difference: She sold the *Daily Worker* (the Communist party newspaper) at twelve, but, confronted by the despair of the unemployed, felt presumptuous. She broke off an important friendship, feeling her mother had been slighted, however unwittingly. As a nurse in blacked-out London, she visited the Cafe Royal and met the unlikely characters found there in those days. She volunteered as a model in return for painting instruction, but in the artist Kokoscha's waiting room, suddenly felt her vocation to be a poet, not a painter, and backed out.

Out of this tension of differences emerged the poems that made Denise Levertov famous. As she wrote so poignantly in her essay, "Autobiographical Sketch":

> Sometimes the poems one is able to write, and the needs and possibilities of day-to-day life, remain separate from each other. One is in despair over the current manifestation of malevolent imbecility and the seemingly invincible power of rapacity, yet finds oneself writing a poem about the trout lilies in the spring woods.[2]

What Denise wanted us to know of her early life, things she did not incarnate in her poems, she put in *Tesserae, Memories, and Suppositions,* which she published two years before her death. Of this work, the English poet Herbert Lomas comments, "She's made herself into an enchanting child, but the art seems neither contrived nor narcissistic."[3]

The "enchanting child" in Denise accompanied her into her seventies, as I witnessed when she gleefully showed me the "sock monkey" she carried with her wherever she traveled. It was her "Teddy Bear" in which she delighted, as she delighted in a story of Brother Juniper, follower of Saint Francis of Assisi, found in her childhood book *The Little Flowers of Saint Francis*.

As the story goes, Brother Juniper went to Rome where his reputation for holiness was widespread, and many devout Romans hurried to meet him. In order to lower their opinion of him (for he considered their interest in him wrongly directed away from Christ), Juniper joined some boys who were seesawing, to the shock and dismay of the pious onlookers. Soon disillusioned by his silly antics, the crowd dispersed, calling him a fool rather than a saint. As a little girl, Denise so enjoyed the story that on the cover of her own copy of *The Little Flowers* she drew herself seesawing with the early Franciscan fool, Juniper. This sense of play reveals a side to Denise that we see from time to time in her poems.

Denise's first published poem, "Listening to Distant Guns," appeared in England's *Poetry Quarterly* in 1940, when she was seventeen years old, and in 1946, she published her first book of poetry, *The Double Image*. In 1947, she married the American writer and novelist Mitchell Goodman, and a year later the couple moved to the

United States, settling in New York City. Their son and only child Nikolai was born in 1949. In 1956, Denise became a naturalized American citizen.

Denise's arrival in America coincided with an American poetry movement that rejected academic formalism in favor of an open, organic form of poetry in which the notions and images are allowed to grow into their own forms, unconstrained by conventional metrics. Shortly after, Denise herself began to work in these freed forms. Through her reading of and close association with the poet William Carlos Williams, she developed what she defined in her essay "The Sense of Pilgrimage" as "the sharp eye for the material world and the keen ear for the vernacular" that is evident in her first book published in the United States, *Here and Now* (1957).

Though her poetry is often quiet and contemplative, and at times playful, it can be fierce and anything but passive in the face of the world's injustice and inhumanity, in the face of war and torture and prejudice. Beginning with her poem, "During the Eichmann Trial" in *The Jacob's Ladder* (1961), Levertov began to move out of the personal world that had characterized her previous poetry and began to engage more explicitly with contemporary social and political issues. This movement resulted in *The Sorrow Dance* (1967), with its unflinching look at the Vietnam War and its implications.

Both Denise's outrage over the contemporary world's situation and her compassion grew as she tried to picture in her imagination the napalmed children of Vietnam, the 1967 Detroit Riots, the forgotten starving children of Biafra. Always with Denise, connection with others begins with the imagination. She clung to imagination desperately, fearing that the images of film and television would so overwhelm her that she would become numb; fearing that becoming accustomed to horror would leave no place within to connect with human suffering.

Denise felt that language, too, was being eroded by the Vietnam War. Being used to justify atrocities, language had been deprived of the truth and of the imagination, which would have enabled presidents and generals to know what they were really doing. She believed all of us needed to *Relearn the Alphabet*, the title of her 1970 book.

My introduction to Denise Levertov was her volume of essays, *Poet in the World* (1973). The year was 1972; I was teaching English at our Franciscan High School Seminary and trying to learn the craft of poetry myself. Her words were a catalyst to my own writing. Five years later, after the publication of my poetry volume, *Song of the Sparrow*, I received in the mail a copy of *In Cuba*, by the Nicaraguan poet-priest, Ernesto Cardenal. This inscription appeared on the first page: "I thought you might enjoy this book. I have your *Song of the Sparrow* for which I thank you and from which, even though I'm religiously vague (I mean chronically undecided as to what I do & don't believe, to put it with a bit more grammatical clarity) I derive pleasure & strength." *Signed, Denise Levertov.*

At the time, I was teaching Levertov's poems in an American Literature class at our college seminary in Southfield, Michigan. I assumed the book, *In Cuba*, with its curious inscription, was a practical joke the student friars were playing on me. It was not, I learned; and my thank-you note to Denise began a friendship of twenty years that encompassed our mutual love of nature, our abhorrence of war and violence, and an ongoing discussion of matters of faith and religion.

Thirteen years later, in 1990, Denise, my father, and I were together, travelling to Las Vegas to commemorate the tenth anniversary of Archbishop Oscar Romero's martyrdom. We were there to pray and make a weekend retreat with many others at the U.S. government's nuclear test site in Nevada. Denise knew how victims of violence in Central America were honored by everyone's response of, "Presente," when the names of the dead were read aloud. She rejoiced to be able to respond with the same "Presente" for Oscar Romero.

As part of the retreat, Denise and I gave a public reading of her work, "El Salvador: Requiem and Invocation." It was a moving moment for everyone present. Over the years, Denise had become a witness to more than just the craft and art of poetry. We realized that we were in the presence of a woman who radiated an aura of peace in that place of non-peace. Even my father, an ex-Marine of the Second Marine Division's Pacific Campaign during World War II, was impressed with her. As a former labor organizer for the United Mine Workers during the Great Depression, he immediately felt connected to Denise's sympathy toward the rights of workers. Denise and I crossed onto United States Government property and were arrested along with others, while my father remained on the other side of the line, unwilling to cross, but standing at attention and saluting our decision to do so.

A few years before Denise died, I spent three days at her home in Seattle. She read a volume of poems I was working on and offered invaluable suggestions, and we talked of what was important to her, especially her recent embracing of Catholicism. It resonated so well with her spiritual, imaginative, symbolizing soul. It provided her with a sustaining sacramental life that, like a poem, incarnated the spiritual in concrete realities, and made room for her own activist lifestyle.

Denise said once that the role of the poet is to witness—not only to *reveal* the divine beauty, but also to *release* the divine beauty. That is exactly what she did for those of us who knew her by the way she lived; that is exactly what she did for all of us in her poetry. Her words and her presence at the Nevada testing site *released* the beauty and the sacredness of the land we were standing on, which was being violated by underground nuclear testing. And her poem about that event, "Making Peace," *released* the divine mystery—that "energy field more intense than war."

In my last visit with her, I tried to summarize in a poem the witness she had become for me and for many others.

The Last Visit

Like your poems
the high front yard
faces a lake's inlet.

Purple, pink, orange and yellow
day lilies
punctuate steep
steps to your front door
where lamb's ear,
alium, ivy and clematis
cover the earth
beneath fig and pear.
Cloistered with fuchsia,
fern, spirea, and impatiens,
you scan the flowers,
talk of saint Romero,
how he died preaching
grammar of justice,
syntax of mutual aid.
At table we share
olivetta bread, peaches, cherries and
a view of clouds
you say is
Mt. Rainier
real as the line we couldn't
see
at Nevada's nuclear site
and crossed

to **restructure the sentence our lives are making.**
Now I see your obituary,
your death
covered with words
I wish were
your new poem,
another glimpse of
the unseen:
energy field
more intense than war.[4]

The words in bold are from Denise's poem, "Making Peace." They incarnate the presence and mystery of "the Word," as a hidden syntax and energy rewriting our world.

CHAPTER 3

Denise Levertov's Prayerful Poetry

In an essay entitled, "A Poet's View," Levertov writes that the "acknowledgement and celebration of mystery probably constitutes the most consistent theme of my poetry from its very beginnings."[1] And for her the way into the mystery is primarily through the imagination, "the chief of human faculties. I would say the imagination, which synergizes intellect, emotion, and instinct, is the perceptive organ through which it is possible, though not inevitable, to experience God."[2]

From Words to Poems

The way Levertov employs the imagination is already mapped out in 1958 in the title poem from her book, *Overland to the Islands*:

Let's go—much as that dog goes,
intently haphazard….
—dancing
edgeways, there's nothing

the dog disdains on his way,
nevertheless he
keeps moving, changing
pace and approach but
not direction—'every step an arrival.'[3]

The dog engaged in its perceptions, disdaining noth-
ing on its way, moving, changing pace and approach but
not direction, with every step being an arrival, is an apt
image of Denise Levertov's life-work as a poet. Because
she is a poet, Denise's perceptions are those of words. She
sees with words; words make her poems. For her a poem
is verbal, musical, structured—a work that enables both
poet and reader to contemplate the experience embod-
ied in the poem itself. The experience of the poem is not
necessarily the experience that triggered the poem, but a
new experience in itself, which is the poem. We all have
experiences we wish we could name or explain. A poet
does this naming and explaining, and if it is done well,
we recognize either our own experience or a new experi-
ence we share together in the poem.

For Levertov, well-chosen words find their own order
in a poem. This trust in words finding their own order is
what makes Levertov's poetry accessible and what gives

her lines their natural conversational sound. Her work also bespeaks the order of close observation: the lines move quite naturally, as the inner eye sees and the inner ear hears. Her line-breaks are often those of the human breath itself as it pauses with the sense of a thought or experience. To read Levertov's poems, then, is to learn to breathe a line, to pause, to reverence the white spaces on the page, and, therefore, to slow down and move with the rhythm of the poem and its line-breaks.

A poem is actually the structured memory of an experience. Following the order of the words, slowing down, breathing with the line, pausing, becoming aware of the space on the page—all these gestures lead the reader or hearer into contemplation of the poem. Poetry is a verbal "going overland," much as the dog goes, "intently haphazard," the light making ripples on his black gleaming fur, a radiance consorting with dance; and in the end this going becomes for Levertov a journey into God through embracing all of creation, disdaining nothing that comes forth from God.

From Poems to Contemplation

Denise's volume *Breathing the Water* (1987) begins with the poem, "Variation on a Theme by Rilke," and ends with, "Variation and Reflection on a Theme by Rilke." She had written elsewhere of the modern German poet, Rainer Maria Rilke:

> His reverence for the "savor of creation,"... leads him to concrete and sensuous images. His passion for "inseeing" leads him to delight, terror, transformation, and the internalization (or absorption) of experience. And his comprehensiveness, which makes no distinction between meeting art and meeting life, shows the poet a way to bridge the gap between the conduct of living and the conduct of art. Because he articulated a view of the poet's role that has not lost its significance as I have read and reread Rilke's prose for almost four decades, he remains a mentor for me now as he was when I was a young girl.[4]

For both Rilke and Levertov, thoughts and images are words-become-poems, a way of contemplating, and ultimately a way of praying. Both are philosophers of the concrete world.

As Coleridge maintains, no one "was ever yet a great poet, without being at the same time a great philosopher,"[5] and if the very word "philosophy" means "the love of wisdom," then Denise Levertov, like Rainer Maria Rilke, is a great poet/philosopher. The arc of her work is a movement from close attention to the natural world, to the wisdom that derives from her observation-become-contemplation.

By Denise's definition, "To contemplate comes from '*templum*, temple, a place, a space for observation, marked out by the augur.' It means, not simply to observe, to regard, but to do these things in the presence of a god."[6] She describes the inception of a poem (and also the vocation of a poet!) again using sacred language:

> [To] meditate is "to keep the mind in a state of contemplation"; its synonym is to "muse," and to muse comes from a word meaning "to stand with open mouth"—not so comical if we think of "inspiration"—to breathe in. So—as the poet stands open-mouthed in the temple of life, contemplating his experience, there come to him the first words of the poem: the words which are to be his way into the poem, if there is to be a poem.[7]

Denise's books record the poems of her open-mouthed contemplation. Every poem issues from her obedience to the discipline of contemplation. *Breathing the Water* both in its title and content illustrates how Denise envisions the creative process and how she makes poems. Her poetry evidences a tension between action and contemplation inherent in the act of seeing; a tension that becomes evident when the poet re-makes something remembered and imagined. "Things" invite contemplation; contemplation then leads to the act of making, which becomes again contemplation of what is made. And for Denise, all this processing takes place not in eternity, but in time.

In "Variation on a Theme by Rilke," both theme and tension are set in time:

A certain day became a presence to me;
…The day's blow
rang out, metallic—or it was I, a bell awakened,
and what I heard was my whole self
saying and singing what it knew: **I can**.[8]

I can—only because "a certain day" has become "a presence to me" that is not static, but a suffered "blow." There is a sense of anointing here, as if a sword were touching the shoulder of a knight-to-be, a sense of awakening to a task. This task could well be the deepening of the experience of awakening and the articulation of this experience in this very poem.

There is in Levertov a receptivity to the wonder of what surrounds her. Here, the day itself seems to be calling her to respond, anointing her for her task of simply responding to this particular day, of saying, *yes I can respond, I can sing, I can consciously embrace this day with honor and a sense of duty in order to live it to the full.* This whole-souled response to the very being of the day is the beginning of all prayer. It is an echo of God's Sabbath rest, saying, *yes, it is good.* But there is more than acknowledgment and gratitude in Levertov's poem. There is also a sense of vocation, a task to be done, even if only that of simply singing out, **I can.**

Can what, though? Live one more day? Celebrate the day? Respond to day as to whoever is anointing me, so that I continue believing I can make a difference by discovering what the day summons me to? All of these are contained in the words, **I can.** This sense of gift, that each day is another summons to be fully human, to be fully responsive to life, is the gift of contemplation, of looking steadfastly and carefully at each day's revelation.

Re-Entering our Experiences

In her poem, "Hunting the Phoenix," Levertov's reimagining the myth of the phoenix, a bird that emerges from its own ashes clarifies the kind of action that flows from contemplation. In the original phoenix myth, a great bird resembling an eagle lives for 500 years, then burns itself up on a pyre of its own making. From the ashes emerges a new bird, thus becoming a symbol of death and resurrection. In Levertov's poem, the narrator is a writer who leafs through "discolored manuscripts" to assure herself there are no words still waiting to be rescued. But she finds "only half-articulated" moments that "play 'statue'" and have not been "released." They haven't been released because:

> You must seek
> the ashy nest itself
> if you hope to find
> charred feathers, smoldering flightbones,
> and a twist of singing flame
> rekindling.[9]

The search of the ashy nest itself is the beginning of the making of the poem and of inner discovery. The poet searches an experience which might seem to be over, consumed; and then she searches using words, not words *about* the experience, but the experience itself re-entered by means of the words that remake it.

Once, when I was trying to rework a poem and kept tinkering with it, Denise told me to forget the tinkering and go back to the experience itself, the experience that was the genesis of the poem. She was asking me to re-enter the experience with new words deriving from the ashy nest itself and not from repeatedly reworking whatever words that were already there in the poem. As I did this, not only did I begin to see the original experience again, but the words I chose to remember with began to create a new poem—the real poem of the experience remembered.

Denise further expands on this advice in her last interview with the arts and religion journal, *Image,* only months before her death:

> If there's a weak place in a poem, weak because it's sort of vague, don't try to rewrite that passage from the realization that it needs rewriting. Go back to the experience itself and look around you and see what you see—Oh, look! there's a little weed growing between those two stones on this road that I'm walking on. It's got a little yellow flower. I didn't notice that before. Or, what a peculiar stain on that wall. It looks like a goat! You can see all

manner of details if you put yourself back in the place where you were, literally, or at the time of conceiving the poem. It takes attention to concrete, visual detail—not visual alone, of course—sensory detail, that releases so many understandings and releases language that you hadn't planned for, but which is demanded by the need to precisely articulate what you are experiencing or have experienced. Abstractions just won't do.[10]

Abstractions won't do in prayer, either. All of us are tempted to gloss over our experiences and quickly name them good or bad, painful or pleasant. We pray about them and from them, with familiar cliches like "Thank you, God, for this wonderful weather, for all the good things you've given us today." Which is fine, as far as it goes. But when we begin to search the specifics of our experience, of the inner and outer weather of our lives, something less desirable may begin to emerge, feelings we may not be prepared to admit.

An instance from my own life comes to mind. I had prayed intensely for someone who was to have an operation. I even arranged for the operation to take place on the Feast of Saint Francis! To all appearances, the operation was a success, but a year of severe pain following the surgery could not be diagnosed. It was finally revealed that the surgeon had covered up a slip of the scalpel that had injured the ilioinguinal nerve, the cause of the pain. I remember being angry with the surgeon, with Saint Francis, with God. I couldn't explain to myself how things had gone wrong; I felt guilty and blamed myself for not praying hard enough.

Gradually, I realized that I had seen my prayer as a kind of magical formula: if I arranged everything correctly, God would be forced to do my will. I had forgotten the mystery of suffering and evil, the humility necessary for all prayer, the need to surrender to God's will no matter what happens. And then I knew I had to forgive: the doctor, Saint Francis, God, and myself. Once I found the true words to describe the experience—mystery, suffering, evil, humility, surrender, forgiveness—I was able to see the experience for what it really was.

Seeing clearly is linked to finding true words and a name for our experiences: "Thank you, God, for the snow that has quieted this early evening. It has made me stay indoors, where I'm talking with you about my anger over that botched surgery, instead of rushing out to shop at the mall in order to distract myself from the anger. It's good in here by the fireplace, letting the fire remind me of your passionate love for us, even when we turn away from you and blame you, forgetting that it's your will that brings peace." Looking honestly at what we experience helps us to find the words to *truly know* what we are experiencing.

Remembering

Searching the ashy nest also involves remembering, an invitation that appears over and over again in Scripture. This search is to remember the works of God in our salvation history and in our personal lives. It is to search our collective and personal memories to find there the phoenix bird of our own faith rising from the ashes where we may have thought it died. To remember is to re-enkindle our faith in God's works and God's promises; to remember means naming the specific acts of God so that we might be renewed in faith. Poems show us a way of remembering; they name for us experiences we may have difficulty articulating.

Levertov's poem, "August Daybreak," illustrates how one can begin to search even "the ashy nest" of a dream-experience:

I hear the books in all the rooms
breathing calmly, and remember a dream I had
    years ago:
my father—all that complexity, cabalistic lore,
childish vanity, heroic wisdom, goodness,
    weakness,
defeat and faith—had become, after traveling
through death's gated tunnel, a rose,
    an old-fashioned dark-pink garden rose.[11]

Dreams, like the poem, search the ashy nest; the poem, like the dream, digs through the surface of "old loves half-articulated" to find "charred feathers, smoldering flight bones, / and a twist of singing flame / rekindling." Dreams lead to the conscious act of interpreting and interpretation summons us back to sleep and more of dream's retrieving work.

Prayer, too, can be a way of searching "the ashy nest," and poetry helps us learn how to search through our experiences, both past and present, and discover how much has been transformed by grace into "a rose." In prayer we contemplate the events of our lives from the perspective of faith. We search "the ashy nest" of Sacred Scripture, which may have seemed lifeless to us, and then in prayer we hear and see words that give us insight and understanding, that console us. Amazingly, we find these words in the same passages of Scripture we've read over and over, but which didn't speak to us, or which we never noticed before searching through the "old stuff" we'd heard and read again and again. All becomes new when, in prayer, we search out both experience and God's Word, and find there "a twist of flame / rekindling."

Searching and Receiving

For Levertov there are two processes involved in poetry making. One is the conscious act of searching the nest; the other is pure gift: the nest simply yielding up its mystery to the poet, as in the following poem, "A Blessing." Once, a friend saw Denise working well and said, "Your river is in full flood.... Work on—use these weeks well!" But Denise felt that the poet "is not so sure of the river."

Is it indeed
strong-flowing, generous? Was there largesse
for alluvial, black, seed-hungry fields?
Or had a flash-flood
swept down these tokens

to be plucked ashore, rescued
only to watch the waters recede
from the stones of an arid valley?[12]

As it happens in the poem, the friend's words are prophetic. The words keep coming. The poet experiences a period of intense "receiving of words and images" that come like gifts she does not have to work for or earn. Much the same happens in prayer. Sometimes we work hard at prayer, we search the nest of God's Word and with difficulty find wisdom and comfort and understanding; other times, all is gift, grace abounding that comes seemingly without our bidding. However, as with the poet, I believe that moments of unsolicited inspiration come because one is immersed already in the work of prayer; one is putting in time each day to search the nest, as it were.

Levertov outlines the two ways of poem-making illustrated in "Hunting the Phoenix" and "A Blessing." She writes in *The Poet in the World:*

> There is nothing one can say directly concerning
> the coming into being of "given" or "inspired"
> poems, because there is no conscious process being
> described. However, in considering what happens

in writing poems which have a known history, I have come to feel convinced that they are not of a *radically* different order; it is simply that in the "given" poem the same kind of work has gone on below, or I would prefer to say beyond, the threshold of consciousness.[13]

These two processes of "hunting" and "receiving" occur throughout Denise's work, two ways into poems that are themselves evidence of the inherent tension between action and contemplation, of outer work and inner work. Similarly in prayer, there is work going on "beyond the threshold of consciousness" when we take the time to pray. Nothing may seem to be happening, but inner work is happening, though at the moment we may not be aware of it. When inspiration and consolation do come, they come from the Spirit of God working in us which we are able to receive because we have made space for God by taking the time to be in prayer.

Praying with Images

Saint Paul tells us that eye has not seen nor ear heard nor has it entered into our heart the things that God has prepared for those who love God (cf. 1 Cor 2:9). And yet, in our imagination we can approach those things;

the imagination of a Dante, for example, can create a heaven, a purgatory, and a hell that seem real to us; even if the real heaven, purgatory, and hell are not exactly what Dante imagines, the truths revealed in his imagining ring true—we know that his great capacity to imagine has grasped things the mind only guesses at.

As with Dante, so with Denise Levertov. Even that which we do not see can be created by the imagination. In "Window Blind," the poem's narrator knows that things happen without our seeing them; she imagines many trees falling in forests with no one there, not only the well-known tree of the philosopher who wonders if a sound occurs when no one hears the tree fall:

> Much happens when we're not there. / Many trees, not only that famous one, over and over, / fall in the forest….[14]

This unseen place or space that the poet wholly imagines and stands before open-mouthed is also a space that has been marked off for contemplation.

Denise Levertov prefaces several of her poems with the phrase, "From the Image Flow," a reminder of the river-image introduced in "A Blessing." There the river was "in full flood"; in other poems, the river flows on, depositing from time to time images that are rescued in poems. Levertov's concept of images being rescued is an interesting development of her phrase, "inviting the muse," and is precisely the kind of activity involved in searching "the ashy nest."

For Denise, images often come from what we have deeply suffered in our lives and the vivid memories left behind, concrete images in our mind. What has been suffered as experience can be re-entered and remade through poems. A poem cannot merely be *about* an experience; it must re-create the experience, with the poet and reader suffering vicariously in the poem itself. If the poem is successful, it *becomes* the experience it names.

The poet works with images that are integral to the prayer tradition called kataphatic prayer, or praying with images. In the Christian tradition, it is sometimes called the *Via Positiva*, or the *Way of Light*. It is typified by "composition of place" in the Ignatian spiritual exercises, and in the Franciscan tradition becomes what Franciscan scholar Ewert Cousins calls "the mysticism of the historical event." Both Ignatian and Franciscan prayer traditions are rooted in the very historicity of biblical events, activating the power of the soul so that we draw out spiritual energy from a past event by meditating on scenes in salvation history, images from the life of Christ and so forth.

Levertov's poems on religious themes proceed by means of images, often drawn from Scripture. Her contemplation is of the kataphatic tradition, in which images are themselves incarnations of thoughts and desires. Generally, we don't pray well if we don't see well with the eyes of our soul, or as medievals said, "with the eye of the heart." If there's one thing that poetry does, it is to help us see with the heart's eye.

Seeing with the Heart

The Life Around Us, Denise Levertov's own selection of her poems on nature, illustrates dramatically how poetry opens the eyes of the heart. In her poem, "Protesting at the Nuclear Site," Denise explored her reaction to the Nevada desert. At the time she joined the antinuclear protest, she had not understood that her unexpected revulsion toward the desert was not because of its barren aridity, but because of what had been done in the desert's depths—the underground nuclear explosions which had contorted the desert's face into a tortured countenance.

As we traveled the Nevada desert together, I listened to Denise lament that she found the desert ugly, so different from the luxuriant English countryside of her childhood. She didn't want to see the desert that way, and yet she did, and wondered why. She began to understand when she heard a native Shoshone elder explain how the joyful face of the desert of his youth, though austere, was not deformed as it is today. This new seeing moved the poet to want to kiss the desert's "leper face." Writing "Protesting at the Nuclear Site," provided Denise with the heart's eye to see that there was something more than burning sun, sand, and sage which somehow repelled her. Reading this poem does the same for anyone who is open to see with the eyes of the heart.

The movement from what is repulsive…to seeing aright…to wanting to kiss the leper, is Saint Francis of Assisi's own movement of prayer. In his last Testament, Francis writes: "When I was in sin, it seemed to me a bitter thing to see lepers, and then the Lord himself led me among them, and what before was repulsive to me was turned into sweetness of soul for me" (author's translation).

True seeing leads to prayer, namely, recognizing and thanking God for leading us to this insight, to joy in this new seeing, and the resulting embrace of what before was repugnant to us. The movement of prayer is from the heart's seeing…to praise and thanksgiving…to articulated utterances that stumble to speak the heart's gratitude or petition...to silence and awe. In poetry—and particularly in the poems of Denise Levertov—there are words, images, and uttered prayers that help us see the wonder of God's workings, and we praise; that help us see the sinfulness of violence and irreverence, and we are moved to repentance and prayer for God's forgiveness; that break through to illuminating grace in the ordinary, and we give thanks for the insight that has moved us to grateful prayer.

The very first poem of *The Life Around Us*, entitled "For Instance," is a good example of how seeing can lead the reader to prayer. The dynamic of the poem is that of remembered moments when the poet was moved to utter Goethe's beautiful words, *"Erde, du liebe,"*—Earth, beloved earth. One could take *The Life Around Us* and read one poem a day and come away saying, *"Erde, du liebe."* That utterance in turn leads the heart to pray, "O God, beloved God, you who have made so lovely an earth; save her, O God, from us who plunder and rape her, who fail to see your hand in everything that is."

Denise saw with a sensitive heart; she began to do so already as a child. In her posthumously published poem, "First Love," she records how her first remembered experience of intimacy and communion was with a flower. Though still so young that she was barely able to ask her mother what she was looking at, she immediately felt that the flower was looking back at her. She began to identify with the flower, feeling that she was the flower, and that there was something *endless* in their shared communion. That moment, she says, was the beginning of a lifetime search for the secret communion she felt with the first flower she ever encountered.

There is in Levertov's later poetry especially, a numinous quality. Her poems are more like doors that open ever so briefly, giving the reader a glimpse of something beyond and within. It is precisely that "numinous something" that is the impetus for prayer in Levertov's poems. Reading her, we intuit that there is more to existence than what can be perceived and experienced by our senses. Furthermore, we know that this "something more" is not transient; it is an enduring reality and only our glimpses of it are transient, passing. Poetry is that which can open the door for us; faith directs our reaction to the numinous.

For most believers, the numinous is a personal God who has a personal relationship with them, someone who hears the deepest, most hidden cry of the heart. And, therefore, prayer is more than an illusory reaching out to something not there. A numinous poem reaffirms the reality which faith already believes is there. True, not every poem has this quality, and neither does every Levertov poem. But the poems and books mentioned in these pages can truly lead to seeing with the eyes of the heart and can open doors to what otherwise is only guessed at.

Reverence

Another dimension of Levertov's poetry is reverence, a fundamental posture for anyone who would learn to pray. Because Denise Levertov is aware of what she calls "a world parallel to ours that is Nature," the individual things in the natural world evoke a certain reverence in us who would approach the mysterious world of nature. This parallel world transcends the workaday world we live in; and when we attain the requisite attention and reverence to enter there, however briefly, we return to our ordinary lives changed.

Denise would pause in a walk through the woods and look with indescribable reverence at something that caught her attention. Usually she would say nothing, nor did she need to. Prayer can be wordless—a simple, reverent glance that transports the pray-er to God.

The same reverential attitude allows the pray-er to move through various objects of prayer (icons, sacred talismans or objects, memorized prayers...) to the parallel worlds they represent. A Catholic who prays reverently before the Holy Eucharist moves through prayer to the reality contained in and beyond the bread and wine upon which the eyes are resting.

Of course, one needs to learn *how* to look reverently just as one needs to learn *how* to read a poem in order for the poem's door to open. One of my hopes is that this small volume will show you how to read a poem so that its parallel world will open up to you—a parallel world that is simultaneously a milieu of prayer. And hopefully, you are beginning to understand how the very reading of a poem slows you down. A good poem can't be read the way we read a newspaper. It is too dense, its images too multi-layered. We have to shift gears from the fast-paced reading meant solely for gaining information. There *is* information in poems, but it is different from advice on how to lose weight effortlessly, or how to make a better cup of coffee.

Nor is a poem's information easily accessed. As with prayer, a poem demands humility. We have to submit to a discipline and to a way of doing that precedes us, that is in fact as old as humankind itself, as old as God's prayer-poem written in all of creation. And because Levertov's seeing is so intimately related to nature, her poetry ultimately is a reading of what is divinely encoded in all of creation. This is her strength as a poet. This is what slowing down to read Denise Levertov helps the reader to do: to read God's messages encoded and written into all of creation.

CHAPTER 4

Praying with Denise

Over and again Denise Levertov's poetry grapples with faith and doubt, using images of the mind that walk the slippery path of the world's wood, with praise and joy on one side, doubt and sorrow on the other; and up ahead, the barrier of suffering and its incomprehensibility. But even on so slick a path, one can kneel and give thanks for something noticed along the way—something the *mind* sees.

"Caedmon"

Increasingly in her later poetry, it is gift, grace, which preoccupies her mind: how no amount of mental effort can earn faith or trust in God's all-surrounding love. We can only kneel in gratitude when Grace "happens." In her poem, "Caedmon," the dynamic of grace is sketched in lines that are themselves gradual revelations. The story of Caedmon, the first English poet, is found in the Venerable Bede's *History of the English Church and People*. Caedmon is a simple cowherd, illiterate and unable to speak eloquently. Levertov envisions his speech as a stumbling walk compared to the dance of others. In her poem, he hunkers down against the barn door with the munching cows and listens to the dancing words of people outside. And then one day something happens:

> The cows
> munched or stirred or were still. I
> was at home and lonely,
> both in good measure. Until
> the sudden angel affrighted me—light effacing
> my feeble beam,
> a forest of torches, feathers of flame, sparks upflying:
> but the cows as before
> were calm, and nothing was burning,
>   nothing but I, as that hand of fire
> touched my lips and scorched my tongue
> and pulled my voice
>   into the ring of the dance.[1]

The ring of the dance refers to infused knowledge that makes one who has felt excluded somehow now included.

Until the sudden angel affrighted me-light effacing my feeble flame...

And it implies not just inclusion, but a facility with words for Caedmon that makes of talk a dance, so that words become music. Interesting, too, is the insight that Caedmon is drawn into the ring of a dance that pre-existed his own singing, into a tradition of singers—much like him—who were drawn into the ring because of their own listening, their own desire to join the dance. For them, too, it was an unexpected, unearned grace. When we are given prayer as a gift from God, we, too, are drawn into a tradition and circle of pray-ers who preceded us and who live on in the communion of saints, of which we are all members.

"Saint Peter and the Angel"

Levertov sees "Caedmon" as a companion piece to her poem, "Saint Peter and the Angel," in which Saint Peter, by no merit of his own, is suddenly delivered from the prison where he was chained. Unchained, he is led into freedom. This is not only a gift, but also presents a task to be performed, a vocation wherein Saint Peter himself must now be the key to the next door, opening to unknown terrors, freedoms, and joys.

The implication is that receiving a gift entails respon-

sibility. Saint Peter passes miraculously through his prison door, the angel leading him. Then alone, without the angel, he must be the key to others' doors. But his experience of the angel and of his deliverance enables him to open the next door, to be its key. That opening, however, will require more than the memory of the delivering angel. It will entail faith, for there are terrors involved: doubt and the realization that he now must walk alone, that he must now do in faith what was once done for him in grace. Like Caedmon, Saint Peter must also join the dance into which something or someone beyond and above his purely human powers has drawn him.

It happens to some who pray or who long to pray that they are given a grace of vision, understanding, or wisdom which they know is not from themselves, but from a transcendent yet immanent source. It is wonderful, but at the same time terrifying, because when the graced moment passes one realizes all remains as it was, though something profound has happened. What to do now?

The temptation is to try to recreate the graced moment, to bring it back. But one cannot do so. It becomes clear that the visionary moment is a call to conversion, to living out the truth of what has happened. Vision implies action, or in the words of Levertov's "Saint Peter and the

Angel," Saint Peter, once freed from prison, had to resume walking the "roads of / what he had still to do."[2]

One of the important lessons any gift of prayer teaches is that the gift is for charity, for a love which transforms one's own life and the lives of others. Each of Caedmon's words had to be fashioned with love through the gift of words, which had previously been freely bestowed on him; so also with the preaching of Peter following his walk with the angel. Ultimately, Peter walked to Rome to meet his own crucifixion which drew him into the ring of Christ's intimates who, in the words of the Book of Revelation, "have washed their robes in the blood of the lamb" (cf. 7:14).

"The Servant-Girl at Emmaus"

Caedmon's and Peter's gifts led to speech. But sometimes there is given infused knowledge alone, without speech, as happens to the domestic in Levertov's poem, "The Servant-Girl at Emmaus," who,

> in the kitchen, absently touching
>   the winejug she's to take in,
> a young Black servant intently listening,
> swings round and sees

the light around him
and is sure.[3]

The "him" is Christ, and the scene is from a painting
by Velazquez of the meal at Emmaus during which Christ
is revealed to his disciples in the breaking of the bread.

What I find striking in this poem is that Christ re-
vealed himself to the Serving Girl in much the same way
as he did to the disciples, even though she is peripheral
to partaking in the breaking of the bread—she is the one
who *serves* at table. There is an inclusion here that is an
epiphany for us who, like the girl, are not present in the
scene itself. We are not at Emmaus where Christ is being
revealed. We, like the serving girl, simply observe; Christ
sees us looking on, and we are included. It is an image of
kataphatic prayer: when we contemplate a scene from
Sacred Scripture, God draws us in; we, too, are there be-
ing included by Christ himself, who sees us and grants us
the grace of the biblical event we are contemplating.

Imagining scenes such as this one makes the salva-
tion event present and reminds us that we need humility.
We are not there; we are that serving girl looking on, but
Christ sees us seeing him and draws us into the ring of

the dance, the "spiritual force-field" of the event itself. In Levertov's poem, the servant girl recognizes Jesus before the disciples do, for she is truly looking, seeing. The grace of knowing is preceded by the act of looking. Her heart, as well as her eyes, are open.

"On a Theme from Julian's Chapter XX"

In Denise's poem, "On a Theme from Julian's Chapter XX" (Julian is Julian of Norwich, a fourteenth-century English mystic), the poet asks regarding Christ's crucifixion, "Why single out this agony? What's / a mere six hours?"[4] The question is: what is the mere six hours of Christ's suffering compared to the years of suffering endured by cancer victims, or torture victims, or victims of drought, or hunger, or exile? The poet's answer is the one Julian writes of in her *Showings*, the book of her revelations or visions, which drew her into "the ring of the dance." In Levertov's poem Julian perceives why,

One only is 'King of Grief.'
The oneing, she saw, the oneing
with the Godhead opened Him utterly
to the pain of all minds, all bodies

❊ ❊ ❊

from first beginning
to last day. The great wonder is
that the human cells of His flesh and bone
didn't explode
when utmost Imagination rose
in that flood of knowledge....[5]

Questions arise: Is Jesus on the cross here an image of
Levertov's own imagination? Once Christ's suffering and
his sharing in the suffering of everyone throughout his-
tory is grasped by the imagination, does this suffering in-
clude the poet's vicarious participation as well? And is
this participation shared by the reader who in turn par-
ticipates through the poet's words? Levertov answers
through Julian of Norwich herself. The suffering Julian
embraced:

To desire wounds—
three, no less, no more—
is audacity, not, five centuries early, neurosis;
it's the desire to enact metaphor, for flesh to make
    known
to intellect (as uttered song
makes known to voice,
as image to eye)

make known in bone and breath
(and not die) God's agony.[6]

Here, the poet sees, contemplates, and then witnesses
to the thing seen through the enactment of "metaphor
for flesh to make known / to intellect...God's agony," or
any other agony. It is the *mind* that grasps, that under-
stands through the enactment of metaphor, which here
is not about mere words but about "bone and breath";
real wounds are Julian's desire. Their imprint in her own
flesh is a metaphor for God's agony on the cross—but
only a metaphor, for even these wounds would not be a
"oneing with the Godhead," as Christ's wounds were. She
would be a sharer in his physical suffering, but not in his
knowledge of all suffering as his "utmost Imagination"
knew it all.

Were Julian to experience in her own flesh the wounds
of Christ, she would know and be a living metaphor of
Christ's wounds, just as an uttered song reveals the voice,
and a seen image reveals the watching eye. Concrete
things become revelations: all things become enacted
metaphors of who God is.

There is a kind of creation spirituality at work here,
as I believe all Levertov's poetry might imply. By this, I

mean a vision whereby all of creation is a great temple in which the works of God are manifested to the prayerful, contemplative mind. In Levertov, the contemplative mind is made manifest in her uttered song and in the images seen with the eye of her imagination. And all this is revealed to us in the way she lets words themselves unfold organically on the page, trusting them to be further metaphors of how her eyes see. Instead of imposing an order on the page, she trusts words to be metaphors of her seeing. In her poems there is a sense of discovery and surprise, as if the very next word (in combination with those that preceded it) will burst forth into meaning the way an image, like a blossom, will suddenly begin to open and reveal the intricacies of its center.

"Poetics of Faith"

The elements of the poetic process as Denise Levertov employs them are the very elements of kataphatic prayer. Levertov herself, in a late poem entitled, "Poetics of Faith," illustrates how imagery becomes meditation.

'Straight to the point'
can ricochet,
unconvincing.
Circumlocution, analogy,

parable's ambiguities, provide
context, stepping-stones.
Most of the time. And then
the lightning power
amidst these indirections,
of plain
unheralded miracle![7]

These lines do concretely what the Church says the prayer of meditation does. It "engages thought, imagination, emotion, and desire. This mobilization of faculties is necessary in order to deepen our convictions of faith, prompt the conversion of our heart, and strengthen our will to follow Christ."[8]

But what do these poetic lines *say*? First of all, Levertov asserts that a mere statement about matters of faith can at times ricochet and not get straight to the point of what a questioner wants to know. And so indirection, parable, story, and the like become ways into the mystery of faith. Metaphor, for example, approaches a point indirectly and thereby gives us a broader vision of the implications, of the overtones of the truth we are contemplating.

For Levertov, that's how we approach matters of faith

most of the time. But there are other times when an insight or inspiration or revelation comes like a lightning bolt, not out of the blue, but out of the very indirections being used to approach the truth. And it is the one who is trying to approach the mystery as best she can, using the tools at her disposal, that experiences the miracle—like Caedmon sitting, listening, trying to enter the dance on his own, and then suddenly being drawn in by the miracle of God's light.

"The Avowal"

Art is the aesthetic organization of the artist's interior journey, successfully expressing and objectifying the artist's interiority. And in Levertov's work, that interior journey was a journey toward faith. She spoke of true work as work that *enfaiths*. And in her case her poem-making did just that. I was privileged to witness her gradual breakthrough to faith, given to me in confidence. It occurred slowly: word by word, line by line, until she could write enfaithed poems.

Denise longed the float and free-fall of grace, as in these lines of the poem, "The Avowal," from her late collection, *Oblique Prayers* (1984).

As swimmers dare
to lie face to the sky
and water bears them,
as hawks rest upon air
and air sustains them,
so would I learn to attain
free-fall, and float
into Creator Spirit's deep embrace,
knowing no effort earns
that all-surrounding grace.[9]

The surrender to God's deep embrace expressed so beautifully here is all any of us can do. We cannot make faith happen by our own efforts; we cannot be certain that God is there to sustain us; we simply surrender to what we want to believe is there: God's all-surrounding grace. And in that surrender is faith given to us.

In an article for *Religion and Intellectual Life*, Denise states, "In the matter of religion I have moved in the last few years...to a position of Christian belief.... The movement has been gradual and continuous."[10] That movement resulted in her becoming a Roman Catholic, both because of Catholicism's deep and rich sacramental life and because she found among her Catholic friends a com-

mitment to peace and justice that she shared and to which she had committed so much of her own life.

The Sacraments appealed to her profoundly. Here were concrete poems: external signs that contained a hidden reality—incarnations of that which they represented. She had seen, from her earliest years, all of nature as a "sacrament" of inner realities, and she found in the Catholic Church a religion that employs concrete, physical things as vehicles of grace. Water, oil, bread, wine, even consummated married love become incarnations of the presence of God.

Within Catholicism, too, she found individuals who were catalysts for her entry into the Church. In an article in *America* magazine, Judith Dunbar writes:

> Denise Levertov's profound respect for Archbishop Romero and others who died struggling against repression in El Salvador were, she told me, among the complex factors prompting her entry into the Catholic Church in the early 1990s, after her move to Seattle. So also was her affirmation of voices like those of Archbishop Raymond Hunthausen and Bishop Thomas Gumbleton, and that of the U.S. Catholic bishops in their pastoral letters critical of

nuclear arms production ("The Challenge of Peace," 1983) and of economic injustice ("Catholic Social Teaching and the U.S. Economy," 1986).[11]

There is a brief mapping of Levertov's movement to faith in the final poems of her last volume, *Sands of the Well*. Completed shortly before Denise's death, it is a slow, prayerful reading of the texts of nature and Scripture. It illustrates through spare images and intense attention to the world around her, how the image of our going along brings us ultimately to prayer wherein every step is an arrival. In fact, the closing series of poems shade gracefully into prayer. Though the nearness of death is felt in the poems entitled, "Altars" and "To Live in the Mercy of God," Levertov is seeing the world without and the world within more intently than ever. She is seeing all as if in a temple; she is in deep contemplation.

"The Beginning of Wisdom"

And from her contemplation come poems that are literally prayers addressed to God. The "I" of the poem is the poet praying; the "You" is God. The poem "The Beginning of Wisdom," begins and ends with the line, "You have brought me so far." In between those lines is a cata-

logue of how God has brought the poet along, making
the poet feel great and small simultaneously. This poem
seems to me a swan song, a modern troubadour's sum-
ming up of her whole life. It is the poem I would place at
the end of her formidable body of work.

The Beginning of Wisdom

PROVERBS 9–10

You have brought me so far.

❊ ❊ ❊

I know so much. Names, verbs, images. My mind
overflows, a drawer that can't close.

❊ ❊ ❊

Unscathed among the tortured. Ignorant
    parchment
uninscribed, light strokes only, where a scribe
tried out a pen.

❊ ❊ ❊

I am so small, a speck of dust

moving across the huge world. The world
a speck of dust in the universe.

❀ ❀ ❀

Are you holding
the universe? You hold
onto my smallness. How do you grasp it,
how does it not
slip away?

❀ ❀ ❀

I know so little.

❀ ❀ ❀

You have brought me so far.[12]

Some prayer talks to God; some prayer listens. This
prayer-poem talks to God, and what impresses me most
about it are not the images, but the long pauses—all the
white space on the page, both between the stanzas and
all around the lines. It reminds the reader that poetry is
not only about words, but about pauses as well, the space
out of which the words emerge. The asterisks emphasize

the context in which the words are uttered; there is thinking here, meditation on one's life, a ruminating heart that needs to wait for the next word, the next line to emerge.

The configuration of the whole poem is that of a map of the poet's life seen from the perspective of old age—all the white space, all that is not filled in with words, all those gaps that have no words. The insights are spare but pointed, crystallized, and addressed to someone else, the "you" of the poem, who is God. It is the way of meditative prayer, this pausing, this slow, deliberate speech addressed to the One who holds onto my smallness.

There is such humility in these lines, such quiet awe, almost as if the song is being whispered. One can hardly hear the tentative, light strokes of the scribe of suffering's pen on the parchment of the poet's life. So light are they, that in comparison to those who have really suffered, the tortured, she feels herself uninscribed. That perspective is humility, the wisdom of the epigraph realized in her own life: "The fear of the Lord is the beginning of wisdom, and knowledge of the Holy One is understanding" (Prv 9–10).

In using the image of herself as parchment being written on by a scribe, and as a speck of dust, Levertov expresses herself in metaphor. The implied comparison of metaphor is the stuff of poetry. Sometimes Levertov's metaphors are condensed to the intensity of the experience mystics talk about when they try to express in words, prayer that has reached the summit of union with God. At other times her images are more diffuse, her language more psalm-like, more like an uttered prayer than an intense experience.

But always in Levertov's poetry there is the reverence, the close attention to God's creation, the awe we associate with the prayerful heart. Her journey to God is twofold. It is a journey by way of metaphors drawn from nature, drawn from the complexity of the human heart with its propensity for good and evil, its conflicts and failures and triumphs, as well as a journey through the social and political triumphs and calamities of her time. Hers is the poet's sensibility, the poet's life, the poet's metaphorical way.

We pray with poems much as we pray the psalms. In a sense, the psalms change valence with each person who comes to them. And the richness of poems and of the poetry of the psalms is that everyone can find a way into prayer by reading them, hearing them, or reciting them aloud. Their music can act as a mantra, a rhythmic in-cantation, while their images act variously, depending on the one who prays.

"Swan in Falling Snow"

The following meditation suggests one way to pray with a poem. I offer it with the hope that one or another point will suggest a way to let a poem lead you into that deep center where you commune with God.

Swan in Falling Snow

Upon the darkish, thin, half-broken ice
there seemed to lie a barrel-sized, heart-shaped
   snowball,
frozen hard, its white
identical with the untrodden white
of the lake shore. Closer, its sombre face—
mask and beak—came clear, the neck's
long cylinder, and the splayed feet, balanced,
weary, immobile. Black water traced, behind it,
an abandoned gesture. Soft
in still air, snowflakes
fell and fell. Silence

deepened, deepened. The short day
suspended itself, endless.[13]

As a prayer-poem, "Swan in Falling Snow" progresses
from outer contemplation to inner peace. The whole
poem proceeds slowly, prayerfully, in the manner of a *lectio
divina*, a holy reading, of the text of the natural world.

Upon the darkish, thin, half-broken ice...

There is something ominous here that reminds us of
how we may have felt at one time or another, perched
upon dark, thin, half-broken ice. The poet does not im-
pose upon the natural scene what is not there. Instead,
she trusts what she sees, names it accurately, and lets the
words of her seeing lead where they will. Danger surrounds
in the thin, half-broken ice, danger hinted at in the word,
"darkish." There is something incomplete; even the bro-
ken ice is *half*-broken.

**Upon the darkish, thin, half-broken ice
there seemed to lie a barrel-sized, heart-shaped
    snowball...**

The poem immediately begins to turn to happier
words, "heart-shaped snowball." Something almost play-
ful enters the poem. "Barrel-sized," too, has that roly-poly

feel about it; something jolly, though still precariously perched on thin ice. The verb here is in the past tense, a subtlety that Denise used often. For Denise, poetry is not something unfolding before her as she writes, rather, it is something remembered and imagined as she writes.

> **Upon the darkish, thin, half-broken ice**
> **there seemed to lie a barrel-sized, heart-shaped**
> > **snowball,**
> **frozen hard, its white**
> **identical with the untrodden white**
> **of the lake shore.**

What the poet sees seems frozen hard—a suggestion of something rigid, immovable. And it is white on white, no contrast, no variety of color, untrodden like the white of the lake shore. We know now that we are looking at a lake and at something barrel-sized, heart-shaped, frozen hard on the thin, broken ice, ice that is the only contrasting color: darkish. The poet is alone, no one has trodden the shore before her. There seems something primal, pristine here.

Notice how no line of a poem is isolated or distinct from the others. Like nature itself, everything in the poem is in relation to everything else, interdependent, an energy field holding all things together. One reads nature that way, and one reads a poem that way. One returns and returns making ever-new connections.

This is a very important point for contemplation. We tend to become impatient, as you may be by now because I keep repeating lines of this poem, going back and including lines we just read in order to get the context for the next line or lines. This is *lectio divina*—how monks have traditionally read the Scriptures. Contemplation and meditation demand this kind of slow recursive reading or looking. The impatient person wants to get on with it, wants prayer to happen immediately and very directly, but it is the slow, careful, patient reader who begins to slow down to the pace with which the poem is intended to be read. Trust that slowness, trust the seeming repetition, the apparent boredom of going over and over something. From the ancients to those who meditate and pray today, we have learned that mantric repetition, and slow, prayerful reading or looking is the way into the mystery of nature and of texts.

> Upon the darkish, thin, half-broken ice
> there seemed to lie a barrel-sized, heart-shaped
>   snowball,
> frozen hard, its white
> identical with the untrodden white

of the lake shore. Closer, its sombre face—
mask and beak—came clear…

As the poet begins to look more closely and draw physically closer to the "heart-shaped snowball," a face emerges, a face that is masked, a face with a beak. Something begins to clarify itself. In Levertov's poems there is always that closer look—that look beyond the obvious facade. And the closer look here reveals the true face of what she is looking at. Whether the face seen be good or evil, tragic or comic is unknown; at this point in the poem we still don't know what this face will reveal. All we know is that the face is sombre, echoing words like, "darkish," "half-broken." Likewise, in our own experience, we often see only dimly at first, and are tempted to prettify or "sugar over" what seems frightening or sombre.

> Upon the darkish, thin, half-broken ice
> there seemed to lie a barrel-sized, heart-shaped
>   snowball,
> frozen hard, its white
> identical with the untrodden white
> of the lake shore. Closer, its sombre face—
> mask and beak—came clear, the neck's
> long cylinder, and the splayed feet, balanced,
> weary, immobile.

Is this a living creature? It has a neck, but the neck is a long cylinder, like a machine or a robot. It has feet, but they are splayed, a word suggesting a water bird but also something blown apart. The whole creature is balanced, but weary, immobile…words that again suggest resonances of "darkish," "half-broken," "hard," "sombre," "mask." A face is emerging, a being we know to be a swan from the title of the poem, but which perhaps we'd not noticed until now, or if we had, we'd forgotten from our position of being too close to see correctly or name the thing seen.

> Upon the darkish, thin, half-broken ice
> there seemed to lie a barrel-sized, heart-shaped
>   snowball,
> frozen hard, its white
> identical with the untrodden white
> of the lake shore. Closer, its sombre face—
> mask and beak—came clear, the neck's
> long cylinder, and the splayed feet, balanced,
> weary, immobile. Black water traced, behind it,
> an abandoned gesture.

You may not have noticed until now that the word "lie" in the second line has a possible double meaning: to recline or to falsify. Such discovery is the advantage of recursive reading, of going back over all the previous lines as you read the new lines. How carefully the poet has chosen her verbs! In the new lines above, for example, black water *traced*, suggests some kind of signature of the creature itself—an abandoned gesture, something left behind.

This is the way to pray a poem, to meditate on a passage—this slowly, this carefully. We miss so much the first time through, not knowing how something read earlier will be taken up again later in the passage, or how something in the beginning of a passage foreshadows what is to come later. In most Christian churches, the Scriptures are read over and over again; we have a liturgical cycle of Scriptures for the year with a repetition of the same text for certain feasts such as Christmas and Easter. Each year as we hear the same texts, we hear something different because of where we are in our lives that differs from where we were the year before. Meanwhile...

Soft
in still air, snowflakes...

A contrast here. Still air, soft snowflakes, with the emphasis on the word, "soft," since that is the word that ends the previous line "an abandoned gesture" and begins the sentence made by the next two lines. Rest is suggested—a rest and peacefulness, despite the bird's now abandoned gesture, which would have been movement

in unfrozen water. The bird itself seems peacefully rest-
ing in the reality of its situation, almost as if it trusts the
soft snow, the still air.

And then the observer wonders whether it wasn't her
or his own seeing that made the scene seem ominous at
first. Perhaps on looking closer, the scene begins to change
because the viewer sees from the swan's vantage point
rather than from his or her own. How often we bring
along our own fears and anxieties to our meditation on
our lives. But if we continue to look carefully and prayer-
fully at whatever within is creating the fear, we begin to
see it from another point of view. Perhaps even as we
imagine God might see it, and all is softened, made safer
by this new vision.

Soft
in still air, snowflakes
fell and fell.

The repetition of "fell" has a feeling of inevitability
about it. The snow will fall, do what we may; it does what
snow does; it snows. We surrender to its inevitability,
abandoning our futile gestures of trying to do whatever
we do when there is no snow, no darkish ice. We leave
the movement of spring and summer and embrace the
stasis, the hibernation of winter.

Soft
in still air, snowflakes
fell and fell. Silence
deepened, deepened.

And that is precisely what happens when we surrender to the rhythms of nature, of the seasons; our hearts quiet down and silence deepens within us with the inevitability of the falling, falling of the snow. Silence deepens, deepens.

Soft
in still air, snowflakes
fell and fell. Silence
deepened, deepened. The short day
suspended itself, endless.

The day is short because it is winter, but it is also short because we have been in deep contemplation. We have been reading nature; we have been suspended in a time outside of time; we have captured a moment that will remain in the poem and in our consciousness forever. A day has become endless by the poet's making it anew with words, and in our entering those words closely as the poet laid them down on the page. Such is contemplation; such is the way poetry leads us into contemplative prayer.

Now pray aloud to yourself this same poem just as you would utter a deeply felt prayer. You will say it differently, more reverently, having now looked at the poem with care and reverence for the words of its making.

Swan in Falling Snow

Upon the darkish, thin, half-broken ice
there seemed to lie a barrel-sized, heart-shaped
    snowball,
frozen hard, its white
identical with the untrodden white
of the lake shore. Closer, its sombre face—
mask and beak—came clear, the neck's
long cylinder, and the splayed feet, balanced,
weary, immobile. Black water traced, behind it,
an abandoned gesture. Soft
in still air, snowflakes
fell and fell. Silence
deepened, deepened. The short day
suspended itself, endless.

At this point, the poem might provoke your own creative meditation. You might wonder, for instance, if the poet, in some region of her consciousness, was remembering that the swan is a symbol of the soul. Was this poem a meditation on her own life?

To see Levertov only as a nature poet, as someone enamored of the natural world, is to miss the essential: she is a poet of the soul and nature is the mirror of her soul. When she explores nature, she is exploring her own soul. Her journey through nature, then, gives us insights into her soul and journey.

CHAPTER 5

Six Ways to Pray Poems

When I began writing these pages, two concerns arose: Would I somehow "dumb down" the poems of Denise Levertov, and by explaining, deprive them of their mystery? And would this section, in particular, seem to be an easy "self-help way" into praying with poems? My experience of prayer both personally and as a spiritual director is that there are no easy step-by-step techniques for learning to pray or for prayerful reading. Prayer involves discipline, perseverance, and a humility that comes from knowing that you cannot control God. You cannot make prayer happen by simply following some easy formula. You learn to pray by praying, and you learn to appreciate poetry by reading it. Poetry is an acquired taste, which is its own reward for those who will read it as carefully as I have tried to demonstrate in this volume.

On the other hand, another pitfall for me as a writer would be to omit this final section. I don't want to suggest that poetry is something reserved for only a few. Poetry is not above anyone; it is for everyone who will surrender to its magic and mystery.

In the steps that follow, therefore, I mean simply to share some of the things I have learned about poetry and prayer and how they are related. I hope that one or more might begin to open for you a prayerful reading of poems as a way into prayer and contemplation.

1. Be Committed

Denise Levertov's commitment to her art was a true vocation. She made hard decisions throughout her life in order to protect and nourish her writing. One conversation we had surrounding her decision to leave her teaching position at Stanford University was particularly helpful to me. As she talked about the years left to her and her primary vocation as a writer, there was no hesitation—though there was some sadness—over her decision to devote the remainder of her life to full-time writing.

I could not help thinking about my own vocation as a Franciscan and as one committed to a life of prayer and service. What personal decisions have I still not made, I wondered, to protect and nourish my own vocation? It reminded me how closely prayer itself relates to the kind of decision-making that a vocation involves.

Prayer is a life-decision made and persevered in, not an occasional petitioning of God. In order to be a prayer, as to be a writer, I must be willing to "put in time," and that involves decisions that are sometimes hard, but which are good decisions for my prayer life. An example of one such decision involves time itself: simply the decision to set aside time for prayer every day. Such a decision is in the end the most important decision one can make regarding an ongoing, conscious relationship with God.

But like all decisions that become a way of life, the decision to set aside time for God each day must be renewed again and again. Otherwise, after a while prayer time becomes simply a time for "getting in" one's prayers—another compartment in our life that we try to squeeze God into. Most of the time, in order to really secure a prayer time, you need to go apart to pray. There must be both an outer and an inner movement that is like entering another dimension of time and space. Ultimately, it involves a restructuring of your life in some way in order to enter a contemplative, prayerful space.

An example from Denise's own life may be helpful here. When she began to commit herself more and more to the vocation of peacemaking, she not only talked about it and wrote about it, but her daily life began to change. She contemplated the horrors of war, the oppression of people, the inequalities she saw around her, and she was moved to personal action.

Denise joined anti-war protest groups; with the Jesuit Daniel Berrigan and her poet friend Muriel Rukeyser, she traveled to Hanoi during the Vietnam War. She joined antinuclear groups, she spoke out against U.S. involvement with oppressive regimes in Central America. And all the while she was writing poems of protest centering on calamitous public and political realities—a radical departure from her previous poems of quiet personal epiphany derived from contemplation of her own immediate world.

The same kind of thing may happen to us when we begin to set aside time for prayer. We begin to associate with others who pray, we attend church more regularly, we find time for retreats and prayer groups. Our life begins to take on the contours of the spiritual world we are committed to. Moreover, we begin to notice injustice around us, and find ourselves reaching out to others. The very external gestures of our life witness to an interiority that was not apparent before.

And this all derives from the initial decision to set aside time for prayer and from persevering in that commitment. No amount of technique, of knowledge of the literature of prayer, no number of spiritual lectures attended, no hours of talking about prayer can ever substitute for the simple decision to set aside time each day to pray. The very act of being in the presence of God teaches what books can never teach. As a poet makes poems by setting aside time to contemplate and write, so a pray-er prays by consciously making time to simply be in the presence of God.

2. Try to Write as a Way of Prayer

I knew before I encountered Denise Levertov's poems that writing can be a way of prayer. Writing had been prayer for me from the time I was a teenager. But what I learned from Denise was to trust my words to take me where I would not have gone without them; to trust the first word to lead to the first line, the second line, and then on to stanza after stanza. Prayer-words will likewise lead to silences and pauses not unlike those blank spaces on the page, those pauses at the end of lines, those pages empty of words, but full of anticipation. And by trusting your own prayer-words to lead you, you will go to places in your heart which were not known to you before you began to articulate your heart's yearning in prayer.

"Making Peace" is a poem by Denise that illustrates how peace is like a poem. I have always read this poem mentally substituting the word "prayer" for peace, especially in the following lines:

> But peace, like a poem
> is not there ahead of itself,
> can't be imagined before it is made,
> can't be known except
> in the words of its making,...
> A line of peace might appear
> if we restructured the sentences our lives are
> making,

❀ ❀ ❀

> peace, a presence,
> an energy field more intense than war,
> might pulse then,
> stanza by stanza into the world,
> each act of living

one of its words, each word
a vibration of light—facets
of the forming crystal.[1]

By substituting "prayer" for "peace," both prayer and the poem are not there ahead of themselves, but are both known only in their doing. They cannot even be imagined except in the "words" that make them, words that in the case of prayer may also be silences that begin to restructure the sentences our lives are making. What a wonderful image—our lives speak a sentence of who we are becoming; or in the language of poetry, words become one line of the poem of prayer that our lives are writing. One line builds on another to create the poem of our life.

Writing itself can illustrate the life of prayer. If you try to write as a form of prayer, one word builds on another, one sentence or line follows another until the prayer emerges. Sometimes there might be no words, but only a blank page created by silence and space. The paper, with words or blank, focuses your soul—maybe a single word emerges, maybe not. But you are in the process of praying, of trying to find words or of waiting for words, of simply sitting in silence, waiting for an image that may or may not come. The writing process itself, then, would be a concrete image of what is happening within you. This is one way to pray, especially for those who find in words a way into the Word, who is God.

3. Be Honest

Denise Levertov was one of the most intellectually honest people I have ever met. She would not say what she did not believe, simply in order to please another. She trusted the truth, and her poems shimmer with a truthful articulation that frees her work from faddish posturing. Her pursuit of true words was lifelong and hard won, a quality that often makes the sentiments expressed in her poems apt reflections of the reader's own unarticulated feelings. Her honesty helps the reader be honest with her or his own feelings.

Denise's words of both faith and doubt speak to God with blatant honesty rather than merely pious thoughts and feelings. Mystic and doctor of the Church Saint Teresa of Avila seemed to have the same approach. I once read that Teresa, after falling from her carriage into the mud, said to God, "No wonder you have so few friends, the way you treat them!"

Factual or not, the sentiments expressed in this short prayer (yes, prayer!) ring true to the ears of anyone who has tried to pray honestly, especially in times of crisis and questioning God's wisdom. Lack of honesty in prayer makes for pious, unreal babbling, not the real conversation with God which Saint Teresa says prayer should be. The reading of good poems not only shows us what honesty looks like, but good poems keep us honest by naming things truly, not sugar-coating our life and the world around us.

God wants our honest thoughts and feelings, as any lover does—not what we're *supposed* to say or feel. The expression of truth binds us to the one who hears and accepts us as we try to be honest; and we, then, are moved to continue an ongoing conversation with the one who hears us. Such is the bond of trust that enables the prayer to speak honestly with God and then to be open to listen to God, in turn—even when God speaks things we would rather not hear: hard truths, hard demands that God sometimes makes of us in prayer. Just as we have felt free enough in love to utter "hard things," angry things in prayer, we become open to what may seem to be "hard things" spoken to us from the Beloved.

4. Plan Well, Strategically

One of my delightful memories of Denise is her inefficiency in doing many practical things most of us take for granted, like changing a typewriter ribbon or a light bulb, or driving a car. I smile, remembering the times she was confronted by a seemingly simple task and she threw up her hands in frustration.

But when it came to those larger actions that so many of us shy away from, she would fearlessly take the bull by the horns and strategically plan and execute a course of action. This was particularly true of action aimed at righting wrongs or raising consciousness about matters of injustice and violence. She spoke of the futility of alerting people to some evil or injustice and then providing nothing concrete for them to do, even if it were no more than signing a petition or praying for the perpetrators or victims. Without a course of action to pursue in the face of injustice, Levertov said, people only become frustrated and angry—another kind of violence.

What then, does this kind of strategic action have to do with prayer? In a word, everything. For, if our prayer is only for ourselves, only for some ethereal experience of God, then it is narcissistic and not true prayer. Real prayer always leads to some form of charity, some reaching out toward and inclusion of others—even if that reaching out is itself in the form of prayer. The true contemplative, for example, embraces God in all of creation, prays for and with all people, and tries to make some difference for good, even if only by praying in a way that includes everyone and all of creation. To pray is to love even your enemy as yourself, to *live* the Ten Commandments, to *live* the Gospel.

Reading Denise Levertov's poetry, one begins to feel with her, to experience and see what she sees. Thus, as your own world begins to expand, your own need to embrace something beyond yourself is awakened; your experience of prayer gives you the energy to respond in action.

5. Believe in Memory

In his *Letters to a Young Poet*, Rainer Maria Rilke encourages his young correspondent to look to his own ordinary life for inspiration. If his life seems poor, it is so only because the young man cannot see and draw from it the riches that are there. And even if the young man were to be in prison, says Rilke, he would have his whole childhood to draw upon, and that memory would suffice for poem-making.

There is about the very idea of childhood a light of innocence and exploration, of first experiences that are formative and that remain embedded in the memory as pivotal experiences, defining who we are and how we see the world. Such exploration is the dynamic of meditation that saints and poets return to again and again in order to remember God's saving work in their lives.

The injunction, "Remember," is one of the most frequent exhortations in the Bible, for it is in remembering the works of God that we are able to define who we are and see the world around us with God's eyes. One has only to think of Saint Paul returning again and again to the memory of his first awareness of God's plan for him and all of creation. He begins every letter with the memory of his own call. His Letter to the Romans begins: "From Paul, servant of Christ Jesus, apostle by God's call, set apart for the service of the Gospel" (Rom 1:1). His Letter to the Ephesians opens with: "Praise be to the God and Father of our Lord Jesus Christ, who has blessed us in the heavenly realms with every spiritual blessing in Christ. For he chose us in him before the creation of the world to be holy and blameless in his sight" (Eph 1:3–5).

To fail to remember is to cut off the most important source of prayer: namely, the realization that God's action always precedes our own, and that God has first loved us (cf. 1 Jn 4:19). And nature reminds us again and again of how God's love is made manifest in the world around us.

In our first innocence—provided of course that we were allowed a childhood—we encountered God's world in all its freshness; and it is the poet who takes us back to that "once upon a time" and helps us see it again. In that re-seeing, we are moved to gratitude and praise, and prayer rises in our hearts. Over and again I return to Denise's poems to see how she remembers and in order to remind myself to keep looking at the world in wonder and to give thanks and praise to so good a God.

6. *Know that Faith is a Journey*

If you want to pray, Saint Augustine says, you are already praying. The same may be said of faith; if you want to believe, you are already on the way to faith. For faith is a gift given to those who are open to receiving it.

If you are afraid to doubt or to struggle with faith, then prayer becomes a pious defense mechanism which prevents you from giving reasons for the faith that is within (cf. 1 Pt 3:15). To struggle with faith is itself a kind of faith. It is to admit that there is something to struggle with—namely faith itself—just as Jacob's wrestling with the angel was an acknowledgement that there was an angel to wrestle with.

Denise spoke periodically of her admiration of those who seemingly lived a faith that she herself could only struggle to let unfold in her life, the way a poem unfolds, line by line, image by image. She realized that faith is a gift, a gift that she saw working in her mother and father's lives. She admired her mother's identification with the biblical lines in Handel's *Messiah*, "I *know* that my Redeemer liveth" (cf. Jb 19:25). That *knowing* was to Denise the kind of faith she wanted. On the surface, such a faith may seem a contradiction, for if we know, we have no need for faith. But the knowing underlined here is to *know in faith*; faith itself gives us knowledge of that which we cannot know without it

Denise's relationship with formal religion was another matter. She had heard much about religion as a child in a devout Anglican home. But already at an early age, she grew skeptical about religion because of her embarrassment over fanatical religious behavior and more importantly, because of God's nonintervention in the suffering of the innocent. She wrote of her gradual coming to terms with these stumbling blocks in an essay entitled, "Work that Enfaiths":

> As to my more substantial stumbling block, the suffering of the innocent and the consequent question of God's nonintervention, which troubled me less in relation to individual instances than in regard to the global panorama of oppression and

violence, it was through poetry—through images given me by creative imagination while pondering the matter—that I worked through to a theological explanation which satisfied me.

God's nature, as Love, demands a freely given requital from that part of the creation, which particularly embodies Consciousness: the Human. God therefore gives to human beings the power to utter yes or no—to perceive the whole range of dualities without which there would be no freedom. An imposed requital of love would be a contradiction in terms.[2]

In addition to her own coming to terms with the problem of suffering, she continued through the years to admire and become associated with Catholics of the peace and justice movement like Dorothy Day, Thomas Merton, and Daniel Berrigan. Along with the martyred Archbishop Oscar Romero, the late Brazilian Bishop Dom Helder Camara was one of her heroes. Denise struggled with her ambivalence toward some Vatican policies, such as those regarding liberation theology in Central and South America. But the example of Catholics who believed and acted out the faith that she herself had come to, as well as her love of the Catholic liturgy and the sacraments, moved her toward her decision to join the Church.

Denise's prayer-to-life was much concerned with peace and justice for the oppressed. She prayed for the homeless and worked for their cause, for example, by giving readings to raise funds for Share Our Strength, a national advocacy coalition for homeless issues. She never closed her eyes to those who live on the margins of society.

The last poem Denise sent me shortly before she died was "Feet." One section of this prose poem is about an encounter with a poor man at a bus stop. The whole poem is a prayerful meditation on feet, which some might consider an unworthy place to begin a meditation. Others, however, immediately connect with Jesus' washing the feet of the Apostles, with the liturgy of Holy Thursday, with Mary washing the feet of Jesus with her tears, anointing them, and drying them with her hair. All these gestures, though lowly, imply reverence and an incarnational view of Divinity. And that is the gesture made by the collection of Denise Levertov's fifty years of poems—a gesture of incarnating the Spirit in words that are themselves incarnations of her seeing.

I am writing these last words on the same beach I walked after hearing of Denise's death. It is the middle of March; the sea is moderate with low swells. Two pelicans fly over my head, gulls and plovers scour the beach at low tide.

Three more pelicans cross my vision as I stare out at the Atlantic Ocean's horizon. A heron sits on a piling, and I think of Denise's love for herons, so obviously incarnated in her poems about them. That kind of connection with Denise happens often as I walk the beach or the Ohio woods or stand before a landscape painting by Corot, one of her favorite painters. That is Denise Levertov's gift: words and images that connect us with nature and art, with one another, with God. That is poetry's gift, and yet another way poetry leads to prayer.

Suggested Poems for Praying

Berry, Wendell
  The Way of Pain

Cairns, Scott
  On Slow Learning

Cherry, Kelly
  Gethsemane

Christensen, Paul
  A Prayer

Clifton, Lucille
  far memory

Deane, John F.
  Out of a Walled Garden: Therese of Lisieux

Dickinson, Emily
  There's a certain slant of light

Dybek, Stuart
Icon

Erdrich, Louise
Saint Clare

Gioa, Dana
Instructions for the Afternoon

Graham, Jorie
Pieta

Harjo, Joy
The Woman Who Fell From the Sky

Hopkins, Gerard Manley
The Windhover

Hudgins, Andrew
The Cestello Annunciation

Kunitz, Stanley
The Long Boat

Lomas, Herbert
Letters in the Dark

Mariani, Paul
One Dark Night

Milosz, Czeslaw
After Enduring

Mora, Pat
The Stations of the Cross / La Via Crucis

Oliver, Mary
The Summer Day

Peacock, Molly
Prarie Prayer

Rilke, Rainer Maria
The Portal

Wright, Charles
December Journal

A Selected Levertov Bibliography

Poetry

This Great Unknowing: Last Poems, 1999

The Life Around Us: Selected Poems on Nature, 1997

The Stream and the Sapphire: Selected Poems on Religious Themes, 1997

The Sands of the Well, 1996

Evening Train, 1992

A Door in the Hive, 1989

Breathing the Water, 1987

Poems 1968–1972, 1983

Candles in Babylon, 1982

Collected Earlier Poems 1940–1960, 1979

Life in the Forest, 1978

The Freeing of the Dust, 1975

Footprints, 1972

To Stay Alive, 1971

Relearning the Alphabet, 1970

The Sorrow Dance, 1967

O Taste and See: New Poems, 1964

The Jacob's Ladder, 1961

With Eyes at the Back of Our Heads, 1959

Overland to the Islands, 1958

Here and Now, 1956

The Double Image, 1946

Prose

Tesserae: Memories and Suppositions, 1995

New & Selected Essays, 1992

Light Up the Cave, 1981

The Poet in the World, 1973

Translations

Black Iris: Selected Poems by Jean Joubert, 1989

Selected Poems by Eugene Guillevic, 1969

In Praise of Krishna: Songs from the Bengali, with Edward C. Dimock, Jr., 1967

Notes

Chapter 1
Calling Poetry...Prayer?

1. *La Divina Commedia di Dante Alighieri*, trans. Henry Wadsworth Longfellow, edited by E. Venturi (Rome: Societa Anonima, Tipografica Castaldi, 1934–XII), p. 573.

2. William Shakespeare, *The Complete Works*, ed. G. B. Harrison (New York: Harcourt, Brace & World, Inc., 1952), p. 1179.

Chapter 2
Denise Levertov: A Contemplative Activist

1. Judith Dunbar, "Denise Levertov: The Sense of Pilgrimage," *America* (May 30, 1998), p. 23.

2. Denise Levertov, *New and Selected Essays* (New York: New Directions, 1992), pp. 263–264.

3. Herbert Lomas, *Private Letter* (December 26, 1997).

4. Murray Bodo, "Last Visit," *Sojourners* (July–August, 1999), p. 37.

Chapter 3
Denise Levertov's Prayerful Poetry

1. Denise Levertov, *New and Selected Essays* (New York: New Directions, 1992), p. 246.

2. Ibid., p. 246.

3. Denise Levertov, *Overland to the Islands* (Jargon, 1958).

4. Denise Levertov, "Rilke as Mentor" in *New and Selected Essays* (New York: New Directions, 1992), pp. 237–238.

5. Samuel Taylor Coleridge, *Biographia Literaria* (XV).

6. Denise Levertov, *The Poet in the World* (New York: New Directions, 1973), p. 8.

7. Ibid., p. 8.

8. Denise Levertov, *Breathing the Water* (New York: New Directions, 1987), p. 3.

9. Ibid., p. 4.

10. "A Conversation with Denise Levertov," *Image*, (Winter 1997–1998, n. 18), pp. 63–64.

11. Levertov, *Breathing the Water* (New York: New Directions, 1987), p. 5.

12. Ibid., p. 6.

13. Denise Levertov, *The Poet in the World* (New York: New Directions, 1973), p. 25.

14. Denise Levertov, *Breathing the Water* (New York: New Directions, 1987), p. 13.

Chapter 4
Praying with Denise

1. Ibid., p. 65.

2. Denise Levertov, *The Stream and the Sapphire* (New York: New Directions, 1997), p. 39.

3. Denise Levertov, *Breathing the Water* (New York: New Directions, 1987), p. 66.

4. Ibid., p. 68.

5. Ibid., pp. 68–69.

6. Ibid., p. 76.

7. Denise Levertov, *Sands of the Well* (New York: New Directions, 1996), p. 110.

8. *Catechism of the Catholic Church* (Washington, D.C.: United States

Catholic Conference, 1994, n. 2708), p. 650.

9. Denise Levertov, *Oblique Prayers* (New York: New Directions, 1984), p. 76.

10. Denise Levertov, *New and Selected Essays* (New York: New Directions, 1992), pp. 241–242.

11. Judith Dunbar, "A Poet's View," *America* (May 30, 1998), p. 25.

12. Levertov, *Sands of the Well* (New York: New Directions, 1996), p. 109.

13. Ibid., p. 43.

Chapter 5
Six Ways to Pray Poems

1. Denise Levertov, *Breathing the Water* (New York: New Directions, 1987), p. 40.

2. Denise Levertov, *New and Selected Essays* (New York: New Directions, 1992), p. 251.

Murray Bodo is a Franciscan priest and a member of the Franciscan Academy. The author of fifteen books, including the best-selling *Francis: The Journey and the Dream*, his poems, stories, and articles have been published in magazines and literary journals. Fr. Murray resides in Cincinnati, Ohio, and spends his summers in Assisi, as a staff member of "Franciscan Pilgrimage Programs."

auline
BOOKS & MEDIA

The Daughters of St. Paul operate book and media centers at the following addresses. Visit, call or write the one nearest you today, or find us on the World Wide Web, www.pauline.org

CALIFORNIA
3908 Sepulveda Blvd., Culver City, CA
  90230; 310-397-8676
5945 Balboa Ave., San Diego, CA
  92111; 858-565-9181
46 Geary Street, San Francisco, CA
  94108; 415-781-5180

FLORIDA
145 S.W. 107th Ave., Miami, FL
  33174; 305-559-6715

HAWAII
1143 Bishop Street, Honolulu, HI
  96813; 808-521-2731
Neighbor Islands call: 800-259-8463

ILLINOIS
172 N. Michigan Ave., Chicago, IL
  60601; 312-346-4228

LOUISIANA
4403 Veterans Blvd., Metairie, LA
  70006; 504-887-7631

MASSACHUSETTS
Rte. 1, 885 Providence Hwy.,
  Dedham, MA 02026;
  781-326-5385

MISSOURI
9804 Watson Rd., St. Louis, MO
  63126; 314-965-3512

NEW JERSEY
561 U.S. Route 1, Wick Plaza,
  Edison, NJ 08817;
  732-572-1200

NEW YORK
150 East 52nd Street, New York, NY
  10022; 212-754-1110
78 Fort Place, Staten Island, NY
  10301; 718-447-5071

OHIO
2105 Ontario Street (at Prospect
  Ave.), Cleveland, OH 44115;
  216-621-9427

PENNSYLVANIA
9171-A Roosevelt Blvd., Philadelphia,
  PA 19114; 215-676-9494

SOUTH CAROLINA
243 King Street, Charleston, SC
  29401; 843-577-0175

TENNESSEE
4811 Poplar Ave., Memphis, TN
  38117; 901-761-2987

TEXAS
114 Main Plaza, San Antonio, TX
  78205; 210-224-8101

VIRGINIA
1025 King Street, Alexandria, VA
  22314; 703-549-3806

CANADA
3022 Dufferin Street, Toronto, Ontario,
  Canada M6B 3T5;
  416-781-9131
1155 Yonge Street, Toronto, Ontario,
  Canada M4T 1W2;
  416-934-3440

¡También somos su fuente para libros, videos y música en español!

THE POETRY AS PRAYER SERIES

offers poetic verse as a means to prayer
exploring the connection
between culture and religion,
creativity and mysticism, literature and life.

Included in the series:

Poetry as Prayer
The Psalms

By Basil Pennington, OCSO
Illustrated by Helen Kita
#5927-3
paperback, 160 pages

Poetry as Prayer
Thomas Merton

By Robert Waldron
Illustrated by Helen Kita
#5919-2
paperback, 200 pages

Poetry as Prayer
Jessica Powers
By Bishop Robert F. Morneau
Illustrated by Joseph Karlik
#5921-4
paperback, 176 pages

Poetry as Prayer
The Hound of Heaven
By Robert Waldron
Illustrated by Anthony Lobosco
#5914-1
paperback, 160 pages

...with more titles to follow!

To order, contact:

Pauline
BOOKS & MEDIA
50 Saint Pauls Avenue, Boston, MA 02130-3491
1-800-876-4463
www.pauline.org
or from the Center nearest you.